German Short Stories

8 Easy to Follow Stories with English Translation For Effective German Learning Experience

Dave Smith

© Copyright 2018 by Dave Smith

All rights reserved.

The following eBook is reproduced below with the goal of providing information that is as accurate and reliable as possible. Regardless, purchasing this eBook can be seen as consent to the fact that both the publisher and the author of this book are in no way experts on the topics discussed within and that any recommendations or suggestions that are made herein are for entertainment purposes only. Professionals should be consulted as needed prior to undertaking any of the action endorsed herein.

This declaration is deemed fair and valid by both the American Bar Association and the Committee of Publishers Association and is legally binding throughout the United States.

Furthermore, the transmission, duplication or reproduction of any of the following work including specific information will be considered an illegal act irrespective of if it is done electronically or in print. This extends to creating a secondary or tertiary copy of the work or a recorded copy and is only allowed with an expressed written consent from the Publisher. All additional rights reserved.

The information in the following pages is broadly considered to be truthful and accurate account of facts, and as such any inattention, use or misuse of the information in question by the reader will render any resulting actions solely under their purview. There are no scenarios in which the publisher or the original author of this work can be in any fashion deemed liable for any hardship or damages that may befall them after undertaking information described herein.

Additionally, the information in the following pages is intended only for informational purposes and should thus be thought of as universal. As befitting its nature, it is presented without assurance regarding its prolonged validity or interim quality. Trademarks that are mentioned are done without written consent and can in no way be considered an endorsement from the trademark holder.

Table of Contents

Introduction 5
Chapter One: Daisy Macbeth 7
Chapter Two: Die Andernacher Bäckersjungen (The
    Andernacher Baker Boy) 19
Chapter Three: Einkaufen im Supermarkt (Shopping in
    the Supermarket) 26
Chapter Four: Unser Haus (Our House) 30
Chapter Five: Die Suche nach Lorna (The Search for
    Lorna) 33
Chapter Six: Der Hausvater (The Householder) 39
Chapter Seven: Das Reiterbild in Düsseldorf (The
    Equestrian Picture in Dusseldorf) 46
Chapter Eight: Der Pfannkuchen (The Pancake) 53
Conclusion 70

Introduction

Congratulations on downloading *German Short Stories* , and thank you for doing so. The German language is a very fascinating language that is at once incredibly useful and feasible for most native English speakers to learn. In downloading this book, the reader can gain an advantage in their communication skills and can also benefit from the innumerable neurobiological advantages which come with learning a second language. The stories featured in this book are at once very entertaining and extremely meaningful, while the tips and grammatical notes featured in each chapter are a potentially irreplaceable asset to any ambitious reader trying to learn the German language.

The following chapters will feature eight selected short stories, presented first in their original German texts followed by their English translations. Finally, each chapter closes off with some grammatical and critical notes on the texts. The purpose of the first two parts is to provide comparative texts for the reader who is attempting to learn German. The last section provides the reader with educational resources for deciphering all the technical details of the texts. It also offers brief plot outlines.

The mention of the German short story genre may harken the educated reader back to the stereotypically doldrum nature of *The Grimm's Fairy Tales* or other similar collections, but none of such stories have been included in this book. The tales featured here are written on a more contemporary note, making them more useful and relevant to the modern reader and learner. It may be noted that the objective of this book is to provide the most relevant information possible to the casual and modern learner. In this book, you will find none of the esoteric verbiages meant for the professional linguist's consumption.

To that end, this book will provide information useful for the beginner or intermediate learner. It is also an entertaining depository of some of the better literature that the German people have to offer; a big task, but one which has been undertaken regardless. As was mentioned before, this book includes eight German short stories. Their titles are as follows: "Daisy Macbeth" by Crystal Jones, "Die Andernacher Bäckersjungen" by H.A. Guerber, "Einkaufen im Supermarkt" (Anonymous), "Unser Haus" (Anonymous), "Die Suche Nach Lorna" by Crystal Jones, "Der Hausvater" by H.A. Guerber, "Das Reiterbild in Düsseldorf" by H.A. Guerber, and "Der Pfannkuchen" by H.A. Guerber.

Chapter One: Daisy Macbeth

German text:

Daisy schaute die Kleider im Schaufenster von Bronzettis Lieblingseis mit drei Geschmacksrichtungen. Sie ging nie in den Laden, ihre Preise waren zu hoch für sie.

"Ich muss zugeben, dass italienische Stile sehr nett sind, aber man muss ziemlich schlank sein, um in sie hineinzukommen," Daisy murmelte vor sich hin. Es war nicht so, dass Daisy fett war, sie war durchschnittlich groß, aber sicherlich nicht hauchdünn, wie die meisten Modelle. Sie sagte zu sich selbst: "Mm, dieser Zweiteiler ist ein schöner Schatten."

Hinter ihrem Rücken hört sie: "Kay, ich habe nicht erwartet, dich hier zu sehen—oh, sorry, du bist nicht Kay, oder?"

Daisy drehte sich um, um zu sehen, wer mit ihr sprach. Es war ein ziemlich schäbig aussehen der, bärtiger Mann im Alter von etwa fünfzig Jahren. Er war eindeutig afrikanischen Ursprungs und hatte einen starken südlichen Akzent. Trotz seiner Kleidung trug er eine Brille einer berühmten italienischen Marke, von der Daisy wusste, dass sie extrem teuer war.

"Nein, in der Tat."

Daisy war es nicht gewohnt, mitten auf der High Street geplaudert zu werden und in Richtung ihrer Lieblingseisdiele zu laufen.

"Bitte entschuldigen Sie, Miss... äh, ich bin Filmregisseurin und..."

"Nein, danke, ich bin nicht interessiert. Auf Wiedersehen."

"Nein, du verstehst nicht. Das bin ich wirklich. Ich bin Lawrence Baker," sagte der Mann Daisy in der Hoffnung, dass die Erwähnung seines Namens sein seltsames Verhalten erklären würde.

"Und ich bin Privatdetektiv!" erwiderte Daisy.

"Oh, das spielt keine Rolle, du wirst genau das Gleiche tun," antwortete Lawrence.

Daisy war ziemlich gut darin, lästige Leute loszuwerden, aber dieses Mal war sie ein wenig neugierig, was hinter dieser Art von Beharrlichkeit steckt.

"Nennen Sie mich Lawrence," fügte der Mann hinzu. "Falls du noch nie von mir gehört hast, ich habe eine Besetzung von *The Tempest* in Harlem inszeniert."

Daisy liebte es, Shakespeare auf der Leinwand zu sehen und hatte den Film tatsächlich gesehen.

"Ich mochte deinen Film sehr, aber ich bin nicht Kay und... oh, du hast nicht von Kay Bartok gesprochen, der kanadischen Schauspielerin in Macbeth, oder? Das hast du auch gemacht, oder?"

"Ja," Lawrence Baker lächelte. Daisy hatte seinen Tag gemacht. "Ich fürchte, meine Filme machen nicht viel Geld, aber es macht mir Freude, eine Engländerin sagen zu hören, dass ihr mindestens einer davon gefallen hat. Aber zurück zum Geschäft. Ich hielt Sie für Kay. Und ich hatte eine wunderbare Idee. Möchtest du für den Rest der Woche ihr Double sein?"

Daisy war fassungslos. Mr. Lawrence fuhr fort: "Dein Gesicht ist nicht genau wie ihres, aber du hast einen identischen Körperbau und nur die gleichen langen hellbraunen Haare. Weißt du, Kay, ist etwas heruntergekommen und sie braucht dringend eine Pause. Die Sache ist die, dass sie in den nächsten Tagen viele Engagements hat, denn wir sind hier, um unseren neuesten Film *Back to the Jungle with a Modem* zu promoten."

"Nun, ich agiere wirklich nicht als Beruf—zumindest manchmal, wenn ich einen Fall untersuche, aber..." sagte Daisy.

"Schau, warum trinken wir nicht eine Tasse Kaffee da drüben," wies Lawrence auf ein Café auf der anderen Straßenseite hin. "Kay trifft mich in diesem Laden, weil sie zuerst einkaufen gehen wollte. Schau, da ist sie, geht jetzt in den Coffee-Shop."

Lawrence war der gesprächige Typ, der nie ein Nein als Antwort akzeptieren würde, und Daisy war ziemlich fasziniert von der ganzen Sache, ihr war nie eine solche Gelegenheit geboten worden, also beschloss sie, Kay Bartok zu treffen. Als sie der Schauspielerin vorgestellt wurde, sah Daisy, dass ihre Gesichtszüge anders waren und dass Kay Bartok mindestens fünfzehn Jahre älter war, aber körperlich waren sie sich tatsächlich sehr ähnlich. Kay Bartok hatte einen starken kanadischen Akzent.

"Sie sind also ein Privatdetektiv, Miss Hamilton. Wie interessant. Du musst dich von Zeit zu Zeit in sehr gefährliche Situationen bringen."

Daisy fand Gefallen an dieser liebenswürdigen Dame, die die Menschen ansah, als ob sie sich aufrichtig für das interessierte, was sie sagten.

"Kay, was meinst du, Miss Hamilton könnte ein schweres Augen-Make-up auftragen, einen Gesichtsschutz-Hut tragen und genau wie du aussehen."

"Einen Moment, Mr. Baker, ich arbeite als Privatdetektiv und nicht als Film-Doppelgänger…"

"Schau, Daisy, wir könnten dich bezahlen, als ob du etwas untersuchen würdest. Du würdest uns einen großen Gefallen tun," Lawrence bestand darauf.

Daisy zögerte: Sie hatte in diesem Moment nur einen Fall zur Hand und so konnte sie einige Büromöbel bezahlen, die sie lange Zeit sehr dringend gebraucht hatte. Berge von Akten waren überall, und ihr Faxgerät funktionierte nicht.

"Nun"—antwortete sie—"Ich wollte gerade in Urlaub fahren, aber ich konnte es für ein paar Tage verschieben."

Lawrence Baker lächelte triumphierend: "Kay, du gehst los und ruhst dich die nächsten Tage aus, und ich nehme Daisy mit zu den Partys und Mittagessen, zu denen du gehen würdest."

Kay Bartok sah erleichtert aus. "Ich danke Ihnen, Miss Hamilton, und ich hoffe, wenn ich das nächste Mal vorbeikomme, kann ich Sie besuchen und wir können eine schöne Zeit zusammen verbringen."

Am nächsten Morgen fand sich Daisy in einer Hotelsuite wieder und Mr. Baker half ihr beim Schminken. Daisy war etwas verwirrt.

"Aber Miss Bartok ist älter als ich! Werden die Leute das nicht bemerken? Und was ist mit ihrem Akzent? Ich klinge nicht wie sie."

Lawrence lachte. "Mach dir keine Sorgen, Daisy. Kay ist bekannt für ihr klassisches Bühnen—und Filmschauspiel, sie hat in London studiert, sie klingt englisch und die meisten Leute denken sowieso, dass sie Englisch ist. Dass Kay älter ist als du, sieht sie in ihren Filmen nicht so aus!"

Daisy nahm den Mut an der Hand und fand heraus, dass sie den Rest der Woche unheimlich viel Spaß hatte. Sie trug schöne Kleidung, eröffnete ein Fest, hatte unglaubliches Essen in wunderbaren Restaurants rund um das Herz von London und verdiente fünfhundert Pfund. Lawrence war einer der angenehmsten Menschen, mit denen sie je gearbeitet hat.

Es gab nur ein Problem—leider hatte sie vier Pfund zugenommen! Zurück in ihrem Büro las Daisy die Zeitungen durch, die sie in den letzten Tagen nicht gelesen hatte. Eine Boulevardzeitung las: "Kay Bartok eröffnet ein Fest im Herzen Englands, um Geld für eine Wohltätigkeitsorganisation für Multiple Sklerose zu sammeln. Fast das Doppelte der erwarteten Summe wurde dank dem Charme dieser großen Schauspielerin gespendet. Es wurde festgestellt, dass sie sehr gut aussah, und noch jünger, als sie aussah, als sie Lady Macbeth in Lawrence Baker's Film spielte. Sie sagte bescheiden, dass sie hofft, in ihrer nächsten Rolle noch besser zu spielen und dass sie englisches Eis sehr mag!"

English text:

While having a nice three-flavor ice cream, Daisy gazed at the clothes past the display window of Bronzetti's. She could never go inside the shop though; their prices were too high for her.

"I must admit that Italian styles are very nice, but you have to be pretty slim to get into them," Daisy mused. She was by no means fat, but nor was she skinny. She had a completely average build. Standing there, she thought: "My, doesn't that two-piece have a lovely color."

Behind her, she hears: "Kay, I wasn't expecting to find you here this early—oh, excuse me, I don't think you're Kay, but perhaps you are?"

Daisy looked behind her to see whose voice it was that she was hearing. It was a somewhat rough-looking, bearded man who appeared to be around fifty years of age. He had a dark complection and sounded like he was from one of the southern states. Despite how modest his clothing looked, he was sporting a famous make of Italian designer glasses, ones she knew to be extremely expensive.

"No, indeed."

Being suddenly spoken to on High Street was not something she was used to, and she made to walk off toward her favourite ice cream shop.

"Please excuse me, Miss... er, you see, I'm a film director and..."

"No, thank you, I'm not interested. Goodbye."

"No, you don't understand. I really am. I'm Lawrence Baker," said the man to Daisy, hoping that the mention of his name would explain his strange behavior.

"And I'm a private investigator!" Daisy retorted.

"Oh, that doesn't matter, you'll do just the same," replied Lawrence.

Daisy was fairly good at shaking off people who look like trouble, but Lawrence's persistence was making her more and more curious.

"My name is Lawrence," the man went on. "Look, in case you've never heard of me, I directed an all-Harlem cast of *The Tempest*."

Daisy had seen Shakespeare on film and had loved it. "Well, I liked your film immensely, but I'm not Kay and... oh, you weren't talking about Kay Bartok, the Canadian actress in *Macbeth*, were you? That was also your film, was it not?

"Yes, it was," Lawrence Baker answered with an amicable smile. It would seem Daisy had made him so very happy. "While my films make very little money, it still gives me pleasure to hear an Englishwoman saying she enjoyed at least one of them. But back to business. I mistook you for Kay. And I've had a wonderful idea. How would you like to be her double for the rest of the week?"

Daisy was nonplussed while Mr. Lawrence went on speaking: "While your face is somewhat dissimilar to hers, you still have a nearly identical build and very similar long brown hair. You know, Kay deserves a well-needed rest. She has been getting a bit rundown lately. She is supposed to be very busy for the next few days with lots of engagements regarding the promotion of our new film *Back to the Jungle with a Modem*."

"Well, I really don't act as a profession—at least, I do sometimes when I'm investigating a case, but..." Daisy said.

"Look, why don't we have a cup of coffee over there," Lawrence pointed toward a small café on the nearby street corner. "Kay is going to that shop to meet me because she wanted to do some shopping first. Look, there she is, going into the coffee shop now."

Lawrence was a very voluble person who would seldom take no as an answer, and Daisy started to become very intrigued by the nature of the events; she had never been offered an opportunity quite like this one. And thus, she and Kay Bartok met. When she and the actress were finally introduced, Daisy noticed that the two had different features and that Kay Bartok appeared to be around fifteen years older than she. But physically, they shared lots of similarities. Kay Bartok's accent was a strong Canadian one.

"So you're a private eye, Miss Hamilton. How very interesting. You must find yourself getting into very dangerous situations from time to time."

Daisy liked this lady because she could see genuine interest in what was said around her in her eyes.

"Kay, what do you think? Miss Hamilton could put on heavy eye makeup and wear a face-covering hat and she would look exactly like you."

"Just a minute, Mr. Baker, I work as a private eye and not as a film double..."

"Look, Daisy, we could pay you just as if you were investigating something. You would be doing us a great favor," Lawrence insisted.

Daisy hesitated; she needed to pay off some office furniture for quite some time and this looked like the quickest route to doing so. Her fax machine had stopped working and there were mountains of files everywhere.

"Well"—she replied—"I was just going on holiday, but I could put it off for a few days."

Lawrence Baker smiled triumphantly: "Kay, you go off and have a rest for the next few days, and I'll take Daisy round with me to the parties and lunches you would be going to."

Kay Bartok appeared to be relieved. "I want to thank you, Miss Hamilton, and I hope the next time I come over, I can look you up and we can have a good time together."

Early the following day, Daisy and Mr. Baker were in a hotel room starting Daisy's makeup. She was a little confused.

"But Miss Bartok is older than I am! Won't people notice? And what about her accent? I sound nothing like her."

Lawrence laughed. "Don't worry, Daisy. Kay is well-known for her stage and film classical acting. She studied in London, you know? She sounds English, and most people think she is English anyway. As to the fact that Kay is older than you, she doesn't look very much older than you in her films!"

Daisy acted very courageously for the remainder of the week and found that she was enjoying herself immensely. She got to wear beautiful clothes, opened a fête, and had great food in lots of great restaurants all around London's center, and all while earning five hundred pounds. Lawrence indeed had been one of the most pleasant people she had ever worked with.

The one problem that she faced was that she now weighed four pounds heavier than before. Upon returning to her office, Daisy began perusing the newspapers she hadn't paid attention to these last few days. She came across a tabloid article which read: "Kay Bartok opens fête in the heart of England to collect money for a multiple sclerosis charity. Nearly double the sum expected was donated thanks to the charm of this great actress. It was noticed that she looked very well, and even younger than she had looked when she played Lady Macbeth in Lawrence Baker's film. She modestly said that she hopes to act even better in her next role and that she likes English ice cream very much!"

Notes:

It's always nice to read a story about someone else's experience that is so far divorced from most people's realities, it almost makes one's head spin. In this fun and very readable anecdote, we caught a glimpse at what is perhaps the more casual side of show-business, the vicissitudes of a director's day-to-day routine.

The text is brief, but it also runs very busily along. The reader is put on even ground with Daisy in that the reader has continual pressure put on them throughout the narrative. The author does a great job of maintaining narrative drive throughout the piece, although it panders off somewhat near the end. But the plot aside, let's now take a look at the grammatical side of things.

Let's start by comparing the first paragraphs of both of these translations. One of the first things that we can take note of is the fact that we are in the past tense and will continue to be for the remainder of the text. German verbs in this tense can usually be conjugated easily.

Let's take a look at some personal pronouns in English along with their German translations to get a better idea of how to decipher all these wild new verbs that are being thrown at us:

English
I
You
He
She
It
We
You (plural)
They (formal)

German
Ich/I
Du
Er/e
Si
Es/s
Mir
Ir/r
Si

The very first verb in the story is *looking*: "Daisy was *looking*..." This is a past continuous form of *look*. To get a better idea of German verb conjugation, we will now conjugate the past continuous tense of the verb "look" in English and in German:

English
I-was looking
You-were looking
He-was looking
She-was looking
It-was looking
We-were looking gesucht
You(pl)-were looking euch
They(fr)-were looking

German
Ich/I-Ich schaute
Du-Du hast gesucht
Er/e-Er hat geschaut
Si-Sie schaut
Es/s-Es sah aus
Mir-Mir haben
Ir/r-Ihr alle guckt an
Si-Sie haben gesucht

These are how they're conjugated in the present tense:

English
I-look
You-look
He-looks
She-looks
It-looks
We-look
You(pl)-look
They(fr)-look

German
Ich/I-ich schaue
Du-Sie sehen
Er/e-er sieht aus
Si-Sie sieht aus
Es/s-es sieht aus
Mir-wir schauen
Ir/r-Sie sehen alle aus
Si-Sie gucken

These resources combined should be a valuable asset to us moving forward.

Chapter Two: Die Andernacher Bäckersjungen
(The Andernacher Baker Boy)

German text:

Die Andernacher, die Bewohner von Andernach, schlafen bis spät in den Tag hinein, und am Morgen sind die Bäcker die einzigen, die früh aufstehen, damit das frische Brot zum Frühstück fertig ist. Es gab einmal einen Krieg zwischen Andernach und Linz, so dass diese Städte auch heute noch nicht glücklich miteinander sind.

Da die Linzer sehr gut wussten, dass die Andernacher lange schliefen, beschlossen sie, die Stadt früh am Morgen anzugreifen. Alle ihre Pläne waren sehr gut gemacht, und sie glaubten, sie würden gewinnen. Um Mitternacht verließen sie Linz und fuhren ruhig nach Andernach, wo sie sich früh auf den Weg machten, und zwar durch den unkontrollierten Turm der Stadt. In der Zwischenzeit backte die Morgen Bäckerei ihr Brot, und als ihre Arbeit beendet war, setzten sich die Bäcker hin, um ein Nickerchen zu machen.

Als Linzer sich der Stadt näherte, schliefen alle Bewohner, bis auf zwei Bäcker. Sie waren nicht allein. Sie gingen leise aus ihren Häusern, weil sie die Thorax Beuten auf dem Turm entdeckten und den herrlichen Honig probieren wollten. Ohne Lärm zu machen, stiegen sie die Treppe des Turms hinauf, und als sie ankamen, hielten sie an und nahmen ein schönes Stück Honig. Sofort hörten die Jungs ein kleines Geräusch.

"Ah!" flüsterte einer zum anderen. "Die Wache kommt! Er wird uns bestrafen."

Der andere hörte dem Lärm zu und sagte nach einem Moment: "Es kann nicht die Wache sein. Er hat geschlafen! Er würde die Treppe hochgehen. Der Lärm kommt nicht von der Treppe! Es scheint da draußen zu sein."

Leise, sehr leise, weil er nicht beim Honig Klauen erwischt werden wollte, ging er mit einem neugierigen Gesichtsausdruck an den Rand des Turms. Da waren die Linzer, alle bewaffnet, und die Kinder sahen, dass sie ihre Leiter aufstellen wollten, um in die Stadt zu gelangen und die schlafenden Bewohner zu hetzen.

Die Bäcker, die die Gefahr für einen Moment hätten begreifen können, hatten ihren Moment verpasst. Was sollen sie tun? Sie konnten nicht schnell genug aufwachen und hatten keine Waffen, um den Feind zu brechen. Sofort dachte ein Bäcker an den Bienenkorb. Er windet sich leise zu seinen Kameraden. Dann hoben sie den Korb vorsichtig an, brachten ihn an den Rand des Turms und warfen ihn sofort auf den am Fuße des Turms versammelten Linzer.

In Fallen zerbrach der Bienenkorb in Stücke und flog wilde Bienen, die den Linzer bis sie laut schrien. Während die aufgeregten Bienen den Stadtturm verteidigten, stürzten die Bäcker die Treppe hinunter, zogen schnell zum Rathaus, läuteten die große Glocke und weckten alle aus ihrem langen Morgenschlaf. Alle gingen nun zum Turm, um die bedrohte Stadt zu verteidigen, aber ihre Hilfe war nicht mehr nötig, da die Bienen so aggressiv waren, dass die Linzer in Eile geflohen waren.

In Dankbarkeit liefen die Andernacher nach Bildern der beiden Bäckerjungen und brachten sie unter den Stadtturm, den sie so gut verteidigt hatten. Sie sind hier noch zu sehen, weil die anderen das Helganthat noch nicht vergessen haben und oft von dem glücklichen Eingreifen der Bäckerjungen sprechen. Die Linzer kamen nie zurück, um die Stadt zu überstürzen, und sie sagen noch heute, dass die Bienen die Stadt am frühen Morgen bewachen, damit der Rest der Stadt schlafen kann.

English text:

The Andernacher, the residents of Andernach, sleep late into the day, and in the morning, the bakers are the only ones who wake up early so that the fresh bread will be ready for breakfast. There was once a war between Andernach and Linz, so these cities are still not happy with one another today.

Because the Linzer knew very well that the Andernacher slept late, they decided to attack the city early in the morning at one point in time. All their plans were very well laid, and they believed they were going to win. At midnight, they left Linz and went quietly to Andernach, where they made their way early and easily to the city's unchecked tower. Meanwhile, the morning bakers baked their bread, and when their work was finished, the bakers sat down to enjoy a morning nap.

When Linzer approached the city, all the inhabitants were asleep, except for two bakers. They weren't alone. They went quietly out of their homes because they discovered the thorax hives on the tower and wanted to try the splendid honey. Without making noise, they climbed the stairs of the tower, and when they arrived, they stopped, taking a nice piece of honey. At once, the boys heard a little noise.

"Ah!" whispered one to the other. "The guard's coming! He's going to punish us."

The other one listened to the noise and said after a moment: "It can't be the guard. He has been asleep! He would get up the stairs. The noise isn't coming from the stairs! It seems to be out there."

Quietly, very quietly, because he didn't want to be caught stealing honey, he went to the edge of the tower, a curious look on his face. There were the Linzer, all armed, and the kids saw that they wanted to set up their ladder to get into the town and rush the sleeping inhabitants.

The bakers, who had a moment to grasp the danger, had missed their moment to do so. What should they do? They couldn't wake up quickly enough and had no weapons to break the enemy. At once, a baker thought about the bee basket. He winded quietly to his comrades. They then lifted the basket carefully, brought it to the edge of the tower, and threw it all onto the Linzer gathered at the foot of the tower.

In their traps, the bee basket broke into pieces and wild bees flew, stinging the Linzer until they cried aloud. While the excited bees defended the city tower, the bakers rushed down the stairs, moved quickly to the rathaus, tolled the big bell, and woke everyone up from their long morning sleep. Everyone now went to the tower to defend the threatened city, but their help was no longer necessary, because the bees had been so aggressive that the Linzer had fled in haste.

In gratitude, the inhabitants of Andernach ran out for pictures of the two baker's boys, and they brought them under the city tower that they had defended so well. They can still be seen here because the others have not forgotten the Helganthat yet and often speak of the happy intervention of the baker's boys. The Linzer never came back to rush the city, and they still say nowadays that the bees are guarding the city early in the morning so that the rest of the town can sleep.

Notes:

This is a rather strange text that takes us back to a time when the term "warfare" had an entirely different meaning than it does today. It is exciting, nonetheless, to think of cities enclosed by enormous towers, an entire town on the same sleeping schedule, and the defensive line of a hive of bees all in one setting; it is a much-welcome and refreshing break from the realities of modern warfare.

This is a great story, and perhaps one of the more entertaining remembrances of the wars fought in our past. Another lens, and maybe a more personal or useful one, to read this story through is that of a *bildungsroman* featuring a couple of baker's boys whose duty it has become to defend their hometown against a foreign militia. This could be interesting, but the plot doesn't delve into any greater detail about the boys—or any of the characters, for that matter.

One thing that differentiates this story from a number of the other stories in this book is its more highly developed and broadly pronounced narrative arc. It starts off small, like a crack in a dam, with the town as a whole sleeping in. Then, it grows into a tale of an army trying to scale the tower defending the town, just as if the dam is starting, little by little, to give way. Finally, the dam breaks and floods the entire area as the bees fend off the invaders. Afterwards, there is finally, presumably, peace.

As far as grammar is concerned, this would be as good of a time as any to go over definite and indefinite article inflections in German. They are very important tools for learning any language and are relevant throughout every text featured in this book. These inflections are differentiated by their gender—masculine (M), feminine (F), neuter (N), plural (P)—below:

Definite Article Inflection (*the*)

Nominative (the): Der (Mas), Die (Fem), Das (Neu), Die (Plu)
Accusative (the): Den (M), Die (F), Das (N), Die (P)
Genitive (the): Des+s (M), Der (F), Des+s (N), Der (P)
Dative (the): Dem (M), Der (F), Dem (N), Den+m (P)

Indefinite Article Inflections (*a, an*)

Nominative (a, an): Ein (Mas), Eine (Fem), Ein (Neu)
Accusative (a, an): Einen (M), Eine (F), Ein (N)
Genitive (a, an): Eines+s (M), Einer (F), Eines+s (N)
Dative (a, an): Einem (M), Einer (F), Einem (N)

While personal pronouns were touched on in the notes section of the previous chapter, they were only in the present tense and were listed with no mention of gender. We would be remiss not to explore some of the various forms of these pronouns, which may even exceed the aforementioned article inflections (listed above) in importance.

Below are singular and plural personal pronouns, translated from German to English in this case, in their nominative, accusative, genitive, and dative variations.

Singular Tense

Nominative: Ich (I), Du (you), Er (he), Sie (she), Es (it)
Accusative: Mich (me), Dich (you), Ihn (him), Sie (her), Es (it)

Genitive: Mein, Meine (my, mine); Dein, Deine (your, yours); Sein, Seine (his); Ihr, Ihre (her, hers); Sein, Seine (its)
Dative: Mir (me), Dir (you), Ihm (him), Ihr (her), Ihm (it)

Plural Tense

Nominative: Wir (we), Ihr (you), Sie (they), Sie (you)
Accusative: Uns (us), Euch (you), Sie (them), Sie (you)
Genitive: Unser, Unsere (our, ours); Eure, Euer (your, yours); Ihr, Ihre (their, theirs); Ihr, Ihre (your, yours)
Dative: Uns (us), Euch (you), Ihnen (them), Ihnen (you)

Chapter Three: Einkaufen im Supermarkt
(Shopping in the Supermarket)

German text:

Frau Meier geht eines Tages in den Supermarkt. Ihr Mann ist nicht zu Hause und sie nimmt den Bus. An der Bushaltestelle trifft sie ihre Freundin Frau Schmidt. Frau Schmidt will auch in den Supermarkt.

Frau Meier: "Das ist toll! Dann können wir zusammen fahren!"

Frau Schmidt: "Ja, das können wir. Und danach können wir Kaffee trinken und Kuchen essen. Im Café neben dem Supermarkt gibt es einen sehr guten Kuchen."

Frau Meier: "Gute Idee!"

Frau Meier und Frau Schmidt gehen zusammen in den Supermarkt.

Frau Meier: "Ich brauche Tomaten. Mein Mann will einen Salat. Ich nehme zehn Tomaten."

Frau Schmidt: "Tomaten sind gut. Ich kaufe fünf Tomaten. Es gibt auch Salat."

Frau Meier nimmt keinen Salat. Aber sie nimmt zwei Gurken. Frau Meier kauft auch ein Kilo Zwiebeln. Frau Schmidt will Brot kaufen.

Frau Meier: "Das Brot hier ist nicht sehr schön, obwohl ich es immer noch in der Bäckerei kaufe. Aber die Schokolade hier ist gut. Es kostet nur 50 Cent. Ich glaube, ich nehme drei Tafeln Schokolade."

Frau Schmidt: "Es gibt ein weiteres Sonderangebot. Mineralwasser und Orangensaft sind billig."

Frau Meier: "Ich habe Orangensaft zu Hause. Aber ich brauche fünf Flaschen Mineralwasser."

Frau Schmidt kauft nur drei Flaschen Mineralwasser. Frau Meier und Frau Schmidt gehen dann zur Kasse. Danach gehen sie ins Cafe. Frau Schmidt trinkt eine Tasse Tee, Frau Meier bevorzugt Kaffee. Sie bestellen zwei Stücke Schokoladenkuchen und nehmen dann den Bus nach Hause.

English text:

Mrs. Meier goes to the supermarket one day. Her husband is not home, and she takes the bus. At the bus stop, she meets her friend Mrs. Schmidt. Mrs. Schmidt also wants to go to the supermarket.

Mrs. Meier: "That's great! Then we can drive together!"

Mrs. Schmidt: "Yes, we can. And afterwards, we can drink coffee and eat cake. In the café next to the supermarket, there is a very good cake."

Mrs. Meier: "Good idea!"

Mrs. Meier and Mrs. Schmidt go to the supermarket together.

Mrs. Meier: "I need tomatoes. My husband wants to have a salad. I'll take ten tomatoes."

Mrs. Schmidt: "Tomatoes are good. I'll buy five tomatoes. There's lettuce, too."

Mrs. Meier does not take lettuce. But she does take two cucumbers. Mrs. Meier also buys a kilo of onions. Mrs. Schmidt wants to buy bread.

Mrs. Meier: "The bread here is not very nice, though I still buy it in the bakery. But the chocolate here is good. It costs only 50 cents. I think I will take three bars of chocolate."

Mrs. Schmidt: "There is another special offer. Mineral water and orange juice are cheap."

Mrs. Meier: "I have orange juice at home. But I do need five bottles of mineral water."

Mrs. Schmidt buys only three bottles of mineral water. Mrs. Meier and Mrs. Schmidt then go to the cash register. Afterwards, they go to the cafe. Mrs. Schmidt drinks a cup of tea, while Mrs. Meier preferred the coffee. They order two pieces of chocolate cake, and then they take the bus home.

Notes:

This brief selection is more valuable in its utility than in its ability to entertain. One would be hard-pressed to find such a short writing so chock-full of useful words and phrases to an ear new to German. It's like vegetables for one's body, or Bach for one's brain.

The most important and most easily notable thing that this text has to offer someone new to German is its food terminology. The foods mentioned are listed below with their German translations in parenthesis:

- Coffee (Kaffee)
- Cake (Kuchen)
- Tomatoes (Tomaten)
- Salad(Salat)
- Lettuce (Grüner Salat)
- Cucumbers (Gurken)
- Onions (Zwiebeln)
- Bread (Brot)
- Chocolate (Schokolade)
- Mineral water (Mineralwasser)
- Orange juice (Orangensaft)
- Tea (Tee)

The other very important terms the text includes are as follows:

- Supermarket (Supermarkt)
- Bus (Bus)
- Bus stop (Bushaltestelle)
- Café (Cafe)
- Bakery (Bäckerei)
- Cash register (Kasse)

Chapter Four: Unser Haus (Our House)

German text:

Ich bin Klara und ich werde Ihnen heute von unserem Haus erzählen. Unser Haus ist sehr groß und hat eine Fläche von 250 Quadratmetern. Wir haben auch einen Garten. Im Garten haben wir viele Blumen und einige Bäume. Im Garten gibt es immer viel zu tun. Ich helfe meinen Eltern gerne dabei, den Überblick zu behalten.

Manchmal kommen Freunde und Familie zu uns nach Hause. Wenn sie es tun, grillen wir im Garten. Es ist immer eine lustige Zeit. Im Haus gibt es zwei Badezimmer. Eines der Badezimmer ist für meine Eltern. Das andere Badezimmer ist für meine Schwester und mich.

Unser Wohnzimmer ist sehr groß und sehr schön. Es gibt ein bequemes Sofa. Neben dem Sofa haben wir einen Tisch und eine Lampe. In der Ecke sitzt ein großer Tisch mit Stühlen, wo wir normalerweise essen. In der Mitte des Raumes befindet sich ein großer Teppich. Der Teppich kommt aus dem Iran. Es gibt auch einen Kamin im Wohnzimmer. Das ist eine sehr gemütliche Sache im Winter und schön warm.

Neben dem Wohnzimmer befindet sich die Küche. Ich mag unsere Küche nicht. Die Möbel sind alt und sehr dunkel. In der Küche gibt es auch einen Esstisch. Unsere Familie isst aber lieber im Wohnzimmer. In der Küche gibt es einen Geschirrspüler, einen Herd und viele Schränke. Es gibt keine Waschmaschine. Die Waschmaschine ist im Keller.

Im ersten Stock befinden sich zwei Kinderzimmer und das Hauptschlafzimmer. Ich finde mein Zimmer schön. Es ist sehr groß und hat weiße Möbel.

English text:

I am Klara, and I'm going to tell you about our house today. Our house is very big, boasting an area of 250 square meters. We also have a garden. In the garden, we have many flowers and some trees. There is always lots of hard work to do in the garden. I like to help my parents in keeping on top of it all.

Sometimes, friends and family come to our house. When they do, we cook barbecue in the garden. It's always a fun time. In the house, there are two bathrooms. One of the bathrooms is for my parents. The other bathroom is for my sister and me.

Our living room is very big and very nice. There is a comfortable sofa. Next to the sofa, we have a table and a lamp. In the corner, there sits a large table with chairs where we usually eat. In the middle of the room is a large carpet. The carpet comes from Iran. There is also a fireplace in the living room. This is a very cozy thing to have in winter, nice and warm.

Next to the living room is the kitchen. I do not like our kitchen. The furniture is old and very dark. In the kitchen, there is also a dining table. Our family prefers to eat in the living room, though. In the kitchen, there is a dishwasher, along with a stove and many cupboards. There is no washing machine. The washing machine is in the basement.

On the first floor are two children's bedrooms and the main bedroom. I think my room is nice. It is very big and has white furniture.

Notes:

This is another example of writing that's more redeeming in its practical application than in its entertainment value. The most important takeaway of this short writing is its household terminology. The places in the house that it mentions are listed below with their German translations in parenthesis:

- Garden (Garten)
- Bathroom (Bad)
- Living room (Wohnzimmer)
- Kitchen (Küche)
- Basement (Keller)
- Children's bedroom (Kinderzimmer)
- Main bedroom (Hauptschlafzimmer)

The other very important terms the text includes are as follows:

- House (Haus)
- Flowers (Blumen)
- Trees (Bäume)
- Table (Tabelle)
- Lamp (Lampe)
- Chairs (Stühle)
- Carpet (Teppich)
- Fireplace (Karmin)
- Dishwasher (Geschirrspüler)
- Stove (Herd)
- Cupboards (Schränke)
- Washing machine (Waschmaschine)
- Furniture (Möbel)

Chapter Five: Die Suche nach Lorna
(The Search for Lorna)

German text:

Daisy Hamilton war Privatdetektivin. Sie war dreißig Jahre alt und seit zwei Jahren Detektivin. Jeden Morgen ging sie in ihr Büro, um auf Anrufe zu warten oder die Tür für Kunden zu öffnen, die ihre Dienste benötigen. Daisy war noch nicht sehr bekannt, aber gelegentlich riefen die Leute sie an, nachdem sie die Anzeige in der Lokalzeitung gesehen hatte.

Eines Morgens gegen elf Uhr hört sie jemanden an ihre Bürotür klopfen. Es war eine fette Dame, die ein teures Fell um den Hals trug.

"Hallo, kann ich Ihnen helfen?" fragte Daisy die Dame. "Bitte kommen Sie und setzen Sie sich."

"Oh ja, in der Tat! Ich brauche dringend Ihre Hilfe, Ms. Hamilton. Lorna, meine Kleine ist verschwunden. Ich weiß nicht, was ich tun soll."

Daisy bot der fetten Dame sofort eine Tasse Instantkaffee an und wartete auf die Details. Die fette Dame setzte sich schwer hin und legte ihre große rote Lederhandtasche auf Daisys Schreibtisch.

"Bitte sagen Sie mir alles—Mrs...?"

"Mrs. Edwina Humphries ist mein Name. Ich fürchte, sie

werden mich um Geld bitten—ich fürchte, Lorna wurde entführt!"

"Das ist schrecklich, Mrs. Humphries. Denkt Mr. Humphries auch, dass Lorna entführt wurde?"

"Mein Mann ist nicht interessiert, ob Lorna entführt wurde oder nicht!"

"Wirklich, Mrs. Humphries? Aber ist Ihr Mann Lorna's richtiger Vater?"

"Ich weiß nicht, was Sie meinen. Wir haben Lorna zusammen gekauft," antwortete Frau Humphries.

"Sie haben… Mrs. Humphries gekauft, das ist illegal."

"Nein, ist es nicht, nicht in Indien!"

"Du hast Lorna in Indien gekauft?"

"Ja, in der Tat! Und sie hat mir seitdem immer gute Gesellschaft geleistet." Frau Humphries öffnete ihre riesige Ledertasche, um ein Taschentuch herauszuziehen. Mit Entsetzen sah Daisy eine zappelnde Kreatur aus dieser Tasche kommen.

"Mrs. Humphries—bringen Sie das sofort weg!" schrie Daisy.

"Was? Oh Lorna—ich habe dich endlich gefunden," sagte Frau Humphries. "Du hast dich in meiner Tasche versteckt, du böses Mädchen!"

"Mrs. Humphries. Das ist Lorna?"

"Ja, unsere bengalische Sumpfschlange. Oh, danke, meine Liebe. Nein, ich glaube, ich brauche deine Dienste nicht mehr!"

Als Daisy nach Frau Humphries die Tür schloss, machte sie eine geistige Notiz, um in die Anzeige zu schreiben: keine Tiere, keine Schlangen.

English text:

Daisy Hamilton was thirty years old and had been a private detective for the last couple of years. Every morning, she would go to her office to wait for phone calls or to come to the door and receive her clients. Daisy wasn't all that famous yet, but she did have quite a popular ad in the local newspaper; lots of people phoned her because of it.

One morning, at around eleven o'clock, she heard a loud knock at her door. It came from a larger woman, and around her neck, she wore an expensive fur.

"Hello, can I help you?" Daisy asked the lady. "Please come and sit down."

"Oh, yes, indeed! I need your help desperately, Ms. Hamilton. Lorna, my little one has disappeared. I don't know what to do."

Daisy immediately offered a cup of coffee to the fat lady as the two women awaited the details. The lady deposited her large red leather handbag on Daisy's desk and sat heavily down.

"Share everything with me, please—Mrs...?"

"Mrs. Edwina Humphries is my name. I am afraid they will ask me for money—I'm afraid Lorna has been kidnapped!"
"That's terrible, Mrs. Humphries. Does Mr. Humphries, too,

think Lorna has been kidnapped?"

"My husband is not interested if Lorna has been kidnapped or not!"

"Really, Mrs. Humphries? But is your husband Lorna's real father?"

"I don't know what you mean. We bought Lorna together," Mrs. Humphries replied.

"You bought… Mrs. Humphries, that's illegal, you know."

"No, it isn't, not in India!"

"You bought Lorna in India?"

"Yes, indeed! And, you know, she has been the best company to me ever since." Mrs. Humphries pulled a handkerchief out of her huge leather bag. Daisy looked on with horror as a wriggling creature came out of the bag.

"Mrs. Humphries—move that away immediately!" Daisy shouted.

"What? Oh, Lorna—I've found you at last!" said Mrs. Humphries. "You hid in my bag—you naughty girl!"

"Mrs. Humphries. This is Lorna?"

"Yes, our Bengali swamp snake. Oh, I do thank you, but it would seem I'll no longer require your services, my dear."

Daisy ushered Mrs. Humphries out and shut the door after her, and as she did she also noted to herself that she should add in her advertisement: no animals, no snakes.

Notes:

Naomi Alderman once said, "Beneath every story, there is another story. There is a hand within the hand... there is a blow behind the blow." This humorous anecdote illustrates that point of meta-storied multiplicity all too effortlessly.

One fascinating quality this story has to offer is its tangible ability to turn an otherwise dull subject matter into a far more memorable experience using irony. Irony, in this case, can be defined as a state of affairs or an event that is often amusing as a result of its being contrary to what one expects. The text begins in a contingent, almost geometric way, and with solidarity. It continues on its path until it explodes into something new: something different with new potentialities. It's always nice to read a plot with this kind of vigor, not necessarily offering satisfaction but always offering meaning.

As mentioned before, unlike its English counterpart, the German language inflects nouns, pronouns, articles, and adjectives into four grammatical cases—Nominative, Accusative, Genitive, and Dative. While German is widely known and considered as a language with more resemblance than dissimilarity to its cousin, the English tongue, the native English speaker new to his or her German textbook often has more difficulty with this disimilarity than he or she does with other aspects of the language. That is why it is very important to be persistent in one's independent study of these cases and their peculiarities.

A few tips in dealing with these sometimes disorienting and befuddling rules and structures are as follows:

The Genitive Case

One rarely uses the genitive case when speaking the language. In fact, the dative case is often substituted for the genitive in conversation. But with this being said, the genitive case will remain more or less obligatory in public speeches, written communication, and any other situation that would not freely give rein to informal language. It is still an unassailablly distinct and definitive part of Germany's *Bildungssprache* (language of education).

In southern German dialects, the use of dative substitutions is more common. The same cannot be said of the German dialects in the northern regions (where Luther's Bible-German had to be learned the way one learns a foreign language) as they more habitually prefer to use the genitive. Though it has been becoming more and more common to neglect the use of the genitive case except when it is formally required to be used, many Germans are aware of how to use it and typically do so. In fact, among the more educated classes, it is even considered a minor embarrassment to be caught using this dative case in an incorrect manner. Thus, for those reasons, it is typically not recommended to avoid learning the genitive case while learning German. It has been gradually falling out of public favor for about 600 years, but it is still far from being extinct.

The Dative Case

For the indirect object of a verb, the dative case is typically used. The dative case also focuses on the location of the object. German speakers place a strong emphasis on the differences between locations and motions; the accusative case is used for the motion of the object and the dative case is for its location.

Chapter Six: Der Hausvater (The Householder)

German text:

Es war einmal ein Mann, der auf Reisen war. Endlich kam er zu einem schönen Haus, das so groß wie ein Palast war.

"Ich konnte gut schlafen," sagte der Mann und ging in den Hofe. Da war ein alter Mann. Der Mann arbeitete daran, Brennholz zu schneiden. "Guten Abend, Vater!" sagte der Reisende. "Guten Abend. Kann ich hier in deinem Haus bleiben?"

"Ich bin nicht der Vater," antwortete der alte Mann in der Hofe, das Holz geteilt. "Betreten Sie das Haus, betreten Sie die Küche. Dort finden Sie meinen Vater. Er wird dir sagen, ob du hier bleiben kannst."

Der Reisende betrat das Haus. Er betrat die Küche und sah einen Mann.

Dieser Mann war alt, er war älter als der Mann, der in der Hofe stand und Holz spaltete. Der alte Mann hat Feuer gemacht.

"Guten Abend, Vater!" sagte der Reisende. "Kann ich hier in deinem Haus bleiben?"

"Ich bin nicht der Vater!" der alte Mann antwortete. "Betreten Sie den Speisesaal. Dort finden Sie meinen Vater. Er sitzt am Tisch und isst."

Der Reisende betrat das Esszimmer. Er sah einen alten, diesmal sehr alten Mann. Er war viel älter als der Mann, der das Feuer in der Küche machte. Der alte Mann saß am Tisch und aß.

"Guten Abend, Vater!" sagte der Reisende. "Kann ich hier bleiben?"

"Ich bin kein Vater! Der alte Mann, der am Tisch saß, hat gegessen. Da ist mein Vater. Er sitzt auf der Bank. Er wird dir sagen, ob du hier bleiben kannst."

Der Reisende ging zur Bank. Da war ein kleiner alter Mann. Er hatte eine lange Pfeife und rauchte.

"Guten Abend, Vater!" sagte der Reisende zu dem kleinen alten Mann, der am Ufer saß und die Pfeife rauchte. "Kann ich hier in deinem Haus bleiben?"

"Ich bin nicht der Vater des Vaters, der kleine alte Mann, der am Ufer saß und die Pfeife rauchte. Da ist mein Vater. Er ist da, im Schlafzimmer. Er liegt im Bett. Er wird dir sagen, ob du hier bleiben kannst."

Der Reisende betrat das Schlafzimmer. Er ist ins Bett gegangen. Da war ein alter, sehr alter Mann, mit zwei großen Augen, die weit offen waren.

"Guten Abend, Vater!" Der Reisende sagte zu dem Mann, der tiefe, offene Augen hatte. "Kann ich hier in deinem Haus bleiben?"

"Ich bin nicht der Vater eines Vaters," sagte der alte Mann, der tief in seinen Augen offen war. "Aber da ist mein Vater. In der

Wiege (das Bett eines sehr kleinen Kindes). Er wird dir sagen, ob du hier bleiben kannst."

Der Reisende ist zur Wiege gegangen. Da war ein alter Mann (sehr alt). Er war kaum so groß wie ein sehr kleines Kind und konnte kaum atmen.

"Guten Abend, Vater," sagte der Reisende dem kleinen, alten Mann, der in der Wiege lag und kaum atmen konnte. "Kann ich hier bleiben?"

Ruhig, sehr ruhig, sehr ruhig: "Ich bin nicht der Vater! Mein Vater hängt da an der Wand, im Trinkhorn. Er wird dir sagen, ob du hier bleiben kannst," sagte der alte Mann, der kaum atmen konnte.

Dann ging der Reisende zur Wand. Er sah das Trinkhorn, und es war ein sehr kleiner, alter Mann. Und der Reisende sagte: "Guten Abend, Vater! Kann ich hier in deinem Haus bleiben?"

Dann hörte er den Mann ganz leise sagen: "Ja, mein Kind."

Der Reisende war glücklich. Er saß auf dem Tisch, und es gab gute Dinge zu essen. Er ging ins Bett und konnte gut schlafen. Er saß vor dem Feuer, und er konnte sich gut aufwärmen; und alles war gut, weil er den Vater des alten Vaters fand.

English text:

There was once a man who was traveling. At last, he came to a beautiful house that was as big as a palace.

"I could sleep well," said the man and went to the courtyard. There was an old man. The man was cutting firewood. "Good evening, Father!" said the traveler. "Good evening. Can I stay here in your house?"

"I'm not the father!" the old man answered in the hofe, the wood divided. "Enter the house, enter the kitchen. That's where you find my father. He will tell you if you can stay here."

The traveler entered the house. He entered the kitchen, and he saw a man. This man was old, he was older than the man who stood in the hofe and split wood. The old man made fire.

"Good evening, Father!" said the traveler. "Can I stay here in your house?"

"I'm not the father!" the old man replied. "Enter the dining room. That's where you find my father. He's sitting at the table and eating."

The traveler entered the dining room. He saw an old, this time very old, man. He was much older than the man who made the fire in the kitchen. The old man sat at the table and ate.

"Good evening, Father!" said the traveler. "Can I stay here?"

"I'm not the father!" The old man who sat at the table was eating. "There's my father. He's sitting on the bank. He will tell you if you can stay here."

The traveler went to the bank. There was a little old man. He had a long whistle and he smoked.

"Good evening, Father!" said the traveler to the little old man who sat on the bank and smoked the pipe. "Can I stay here in your house?"

"I'm not the father's father," said the little old man who sat on the bank and smoked the pipe. "There's my father. He's there, in the bedroom. He's lying in the bed. He will tell you if you can stay here."

The traveler entered the bedroom. He went to bed. There was an old, very old man, with two big eyes that were wide open.

"Good evening, Father!" the traveler said to the man who had open eyes. "Can I stay here in your house?"

"I'm not a father's father," said the old man whose eyes were deeply open. "But there's my father. In the cradle (the bed of a very small child). He will tell you if you can stay here."

The traveler went to the cradle. There was an ancient man (very old). He was hardly as big as a very young child, and he could barely breathe.

"Good evening, Father!" the traveler told the small, ancient man who was in the cradle and could barely breathe. "Can I stay here?"

Quiet, very quiet, very quiet: "I'm not the father! My father hangs there on the wall, in the drinking horn. He will tell you if you can stay here," said the ancient man who could barely breathe.

Then the traveler went to the wall. He saw the drinking horn, and in it was a very small, ancient man. And the traveler said: "Good evening, Father! Can I stay here in your house?"

Then he heard the man very quietly say: "Yeah, my child."

The traveler was happy. He sat on the table, and there were good things to eat. He went to bed and he could sleep well. He sat in front of the fire, and he could warm himself well; and everything was good because he found the old father's father.

Notes:

In its narrative structure, this story is very similar to the one featured in Chapter 5, "Die Suche nach Lorna." The main variance between the two is in their conclusions. Where "Die Suche nach Lorna" ends on an unexpected, comical note, this one ends on a very-much-anticipated and assuring note.

One theme that can be considered throughout this text harkens back to Robert Frost's *After Apple-picking*, about seeing life as a series of opportunities. The traveler wanders through the story looking for the father's father, meeting multiple new people along the way. He meets each and every one of the characters in a different location, all with their own unique features and happenings. He expands through his new experiences and perspectives, and after that, he cannot contract back to the parameters previously put around him.

All throughout the main character's quest for the father of the house, he keeps reciting the interrogative: "Can I stay here?"

Interrogative sentences like these are a highly useful and necessary aspect of any language. Learning how to construct these sentences is an absolute necessity when learning any tongue, especially for the beginner or the casual traveler. The construction of these sentences is not the same in German as it is in English. The pattern for constructing these sentences are listed below:

Supplementary Questions

1. Question word
2. Verb (inflected according to the subject)
3. Subject
4. Other sentence elements

Yes/No Questions

1. Verb (inflected according to the subject)
2. Subject
3. Other sentence elements

Below, we have the common question words in English listed along with their German translations.

English	**Geman**
Who?	Wer?
Who(m)?	Wen?
Who(m)...to?	Wem?
Whose?	Wessen?
What?	Was?
Where?	Wo?
Where...to?	Wohin?
When?	Wann?
How long since?	Seit wann?
From when until when?	Von wann bis wann?
How? What?	Wie?
How much? How many?	Wie viel(e)?
Which? Whichever?	Welche(r/s)?
What a...?	Was fur(ein/e)?
Why?	Warum?

Chapter Seven: Das Reiterbild in Düsseldorf
(The Equestrian Picture in Dusseldorf)

German text:

Ein Künstler lebte einst in Düsseldorf am Rhein. Er war sehr geschickt, so klug, dass der Kurfürst seinen Atem ins Erz goss. Der Künstler war sehr glücklich und arbeitete Tag und Nacht. Endlich war ein Bild fertig und Meister Grupello, der Künstler, brachte es auf den Markt. Als es fertig war, kam der Kurfürst Johann Wilhelm mit all seinen Höfingen. Der Künstler ließ den Schleier fallen, damit jeder das Bild sehen konnte.

Der Kurde, erstaunt über die Schönheit dieses Bildes, gab dem Künstler die Hand und sagte: "Nun, Herr Grupello, Sie haben das sehr gut gemacht. Dieses Bild ist sehr schön. Es ist wirklich tadellos! Du bist ein großer Künstler, und das Bild gibt dir große Ehre!"

Der Künstler war begeistert von diesem Lob, aber die Höflinge, die stillschweigend (ohne ein Wort zu sagen) waren eifersüchtig. Der Fürst hatte ihnen nie eine so freundliche Hand gegeben und sie nie gelobt, und sie alle dachten an sich selbst: "Wie können wir diesen stolzen Künstler demütigen?"

Da der Prinz sein Bild beeindruckend fand, konnten sie nichts Schlechtes darüber sagen, aber endlich sagte der eine: "Ja, Herr Grupello, das Bild des Prinzen ist wirklich makellos. Das Pferd hingegen ist nicht ganz richtig. Schau, der Kopf ist etwas zu groß, das ist nicht ganz natürlich!"

"Nein," sagte der zweite, "das Pferd war nicht so erfolgreich, wie es hätte sein können. Sehen Sie sich den Hals an, Herr Grupello!"

"Ja, und der rechte Fuß ist nicht richtig," sagte der dritte. Der vierte lobte das Bild, aber er rügte den Schwanz des Pferdes. Der fünfte war auch kritisch gegenüber dem Pferd, und nach all ihren Meinungen sagte der Künstler zu dem Prinzen: "Mein Prinz, Ihre Höflinge sind nicht ganz zufrieden mit meiner Arbeit, sie strömen über mich wegen der Pferde."

"Lassen Sie mich ein paar Tage an dem Bild arbeiten, Herr Grupello," antwortete der Kurfürst freundschaftlich. "Bitte tun Sie, was immer Sie für nötig halten. Der Künstler hinterließ den Schleier über dem Bild, und als am nächsten Morgen der Prinz und seine Höflinge zurückkamen, um das Bild wieder zu sehen."

"Oh," dachten alle selbstbewusst. "Ich habe dem Künstler einen guten Rat gegeben. Das Pferd hatte keinen Erfolg. Er hat es selbst gesehen und jetzt ändert er es. Dank meines Ratschlags wird das Bild jetzt wirklich tadellos sein."

Als die Nacht vorbei war, kamen der Kurspreis und seine Höflinge ein zweites Mal, um das Bild zu sehen. Das hohe Brett war verschwunden, und als der Schleier wieder fiel, freute sich der Kurfürst. Dann rief er die Höflinge nacheinander an und fragte sie danach.

Die erste Person, die seinen Kopf geworfen hat, sagte jetzt: "Ah, Herr Kurfürst, das Bild ist jetzt sehr makellos, und Sie sehen den Kopf des Pferdes, jetzt ist er nicht zu groß, aber ganz natürlich."

Der zweite sagte: "Ja, das Bild ist jetzt sehr makellos. Der Hals des Pferdes ist jetzt sehr gnädig."

Der dritte sagte: "Da Sie den rechten Fuß gewechselt haben, Herr Grupello, ist Ihr Bild einwandfrei."

Alle waren jetzt sehr glücklich, und der Kurde erzählte dem Künstler, der still war, "Herr Grupello, alle diese Herren sind jetzt zufrieden mit Ihrer Arbeit und loben Ihre Veränderungen am Pferd."

"Herr Kurfürst," antwortete der Künstler, "ich bin sehr froh, dass alle mit meinem Bild so zufrieden sind, aber ich muss zugeben, dass ich daran nichts geändert habe. Ein Bild kann nicht verändert werden. Trotzdem habe ich euch jetzt alle gehört."

Der Kurfürst war überrascht. "Über was hast du geredet?"

"Über den Ruf Ihrer Höflinge, Herr Fürst, der auf der Suche nach dem Bild der Eifersucht war, und ich glaube, das ist jetzt völlig zerstört!"

Die Höflinge konnten sich nicht revanchieren, und sie alle setzten ihre Kritik fort. Das Bild ist immer noch das Herzstück des Düsseldorfer Marktes, wo es jeder bewundern kann.

English text:

An artist once lived in Dusseldorf on the Rhine. He was very skillful, so clever that the Kurfürst "poured his breath into the ore." The artist was very happy and worked day and night. At last, a picture was finished and Master Grupello, the artist, put it on the market. When it was complete, the Kurprince Johann

Wilhelm came to see it with all his courtiers. The artist dropped the veil so everyone could see the picture.

The prince, astonished by the beauty of this image, gave the artist his hand and said: "Now, Mr. Grupello, you have done this very well. This picture is very beautiful. It really is impeccable! You are a great artist, and the picture gives you great honor!"

The artist was delighted with this praise, but the courtiers who were taciturn (without saying a word) were jealous. The prince had never given them such a friendly hand or praised them, and they all thought to themselves: "How can we humiliate this proud artist?"

Since the prince found his image impressive, they couldn't say anything bad about it, but at last one said: "Yes, Mr. Grupello, the image of the prince is really impeccable. The horse, on the other hand, is not quite right. Look, the head is a little too big, it's not quite natural!"

"No," the second said, "the horse did not succeed as well as it could have. Look at the neck, Mr. Grupello!"

"Yes, and the right foot isn't right," said the third. The fourth praised the picture, but he reprimanded the horse's tail.

The fifth was also critical of the horse and, after all their opinions, the artist said to the prince: "My Prince, your courtiers are not entirely satisfied with my work, they are pouring onto me about the horses. Are you going to let me work on the picture for a few days?"

"If you like, Mr. Grupello," the Kurfürst responded amicably.

"Please do to it whatever you deem necessary."

The artist left the veil over the picture, and when the next morning approached, the prince and his courtiers came back to see the picture again.

"Oh," all of them thought to themselves with confidence. "I gave the artist a good advice. The horse didn't succeed at all. He saw it himself, and now he changed it. Thanks to my advice, the picture will now be really impeccable."

When the night was over, the prince and his courtiers came to see the picture a second time. The high plank had disappeared, and when the veil fell again, the prince was rejoicing. Then he called the courtiers, one after the other, and asked them about it. The first person who threw his head said now: "Ah, my prince, the picture is now very impeccable. And look at the head of the horse, now he is not too big, but quite natural."

The second said: "Yes, the picture's very impeccable now. The neck of the horse is now very graceful."

The third said: "Since you have changed the right foot, Mr. Grupello, your picture is perfect."

Everyone was very happy now, and the Kurprince told the artist who was silent, "Mr. Grupello, all these gentlemen are now satisfied with your work; they all praise your changes to the horse."

"My prince," the artist replied, "I am quite happy that everyone is so pleased with my picture, but I have to admit that I have not changed anything about it. A picture cannot be changed. Nevertheless, I have heard you all now."

The prince was surprised. "What are you talking about?"

"The reputation of your courtiers, my prince, who was looking for the image of jealousy. And I think that is now completely destroyed!"

The courtiers couldn't reciprocate, and they all continued with their criticisms. The picture is still at the heart of the market in Dusseldorf, where everyone can admire it.

Notes:

This is a very fascinating story. Anyone who has ever found themselves criticised unjustifiably by others might easily relate, especially if the critics had been remiss to consider the best interest of the one being criticized. Anyone who has ever felt alienated among peers, or perhaps conspired against, will almost invariably take this story to heart. Arguably the most important action of this story is Mr. Grupello's maturity and grace in silencing his pedantic tormentors.

The second half of the story where the prince and his harsh courtiers come back to reexamine the picture begins with the courtiers at last praising the picture. But the love they bestow is ultimately unveiled as an illusion brought on by confirmation bias after Mr. Grupello reveals that he had made no changes to the picture, explaining that "a picture can not be changed."

This really is a great example of what to do when one is being brought down by others who are willing to blow hot or cold at any given thing based on what the others among their peers decide. As soon as the first courtier gave an opinion and took leadership of the rest, the prospect of the painter having a fair trial vanished, and with it went the other courtier's abilities to think for themselves. That is the main reason that this story is a classic, even though it may not be the most well-known story in the world or even in this book. Its content has a relatability in any era.

One very important aspect of the German language is the subject of phrases. This is of particular importance to the native English speaker because German uses a process called declension which English does not. An example of this process is shown below:

Mary reads a book. She reads a book.

"Mary" is the subject of the phrase, and "she" also happens to be in the nominative case. The reader can ask "who?" after the subject of this phrase. Who is it who reads the book? It is Mary.

This phrase's subject defines its verb. Mary happens to be in the third person singular tense right now. If we were to change the phrase into the first person plural, for example, then the verb would change with it as well.

Chapter Eight: Der Pfannkuchen (The Pancake)

German text:

Es war einmal eine Frau, die sieben hungrige Kinder hatte. Sie machte einen Pfannkuchen für die hungrigen Kinder. Es war ein großer Pfannkuchen, aus süßer Milch gemacht, und er lag in der Pfanne auf dem Feuer.

Die Kinder, die so hungrig waren, standen alle da und das erste Kind sagte: "Ach, Mutter, ich bin so hungrig, gieb mir ein Stück Pfannkuchen."

"Ach, gute Mutter!" sagte das zweite Kind. "Ich bin auch hungrig, gieb mir auch ein Stück Pfannkuchen."

"Ach, liebe, gute Mutter!" sagte das dritte Kind. "Ich bin auch hungrig. Gieb mir ein Stück Pfannkuchen."

"Ach, süße, gute, liebe Mutter," sagte das vierte Kind. "Ich habe auch Hunger. Ich möchte auch ein Stück Pfannkuchen haben."

"Liebe, gute, süße, kleine Mutter," rief (sagte laut) das fünfte Kind. "Ich möchte auch ein Stück Pfannkuchen haben."

Und das sechste Kind rief: "Geschickte, gute, süße, liebe, kleine Mutter, laß mich auch ein Stück Pfannkuchen haben. Ich habe auch Hunger."

Und das siebente und letzte Kind rief: "Geschickte, gute, süße, liebe, niedliche, kleine Mutter, laß mich auch ein Stück

Pfannkuchen haben. Ich habe auch Hunger."

"Ja, ja, meine Kinder," antwortete die Frau. "Wartet nur, bis der Pfannkuchen auf der anderen Seite gebacken ist. Seht, er ist so schön und wird so gut zu essen sein."

Als der Kuchen das hörte, fürchtete er sich sehr und drehte sich schnell um. Jetzt konnte er auch auf der anderen Seite backen. Nach einigen Minuten war der Pfannkuchen gebacken, aber da er sich so sehr fürchtete, sprang er aus der Pfanne. Er sprang auf den Boden und rollte schnell aus dem Hause.

"Halt, Pfannkuchen, halt!" rief die Mutter.

"Halt, Pfannkuchen, halt!" riefen die sieben Kinder.

Aber der Kuchen rollte schnell weiter. Die Frau und alle sieben Kinder liefen ihm nach, aber er rollte so schnell, daß sie ihn bald nicht mehr sehen konnten. Der Pfannkuchen rollte weiter und weiter, und endlich begegnete er einem alten Manne.

"Guten Tag, Pfannkuchen!" rief der Mann.

"Gott behüte Sie!" antwortete der Pfannkuchen.

"Rollen Sie nicht so schnell, lieber Pfannkuchen. Warten Sie. Ich möchte Sie essen!"

"Ach!" antwortete der Pfannkuchen. "Ich muß schnell fortrollen, denn die Frau mit den sieben hungrigen Kindern kommt, um mich zu essen!"

Und der Pfannkuchen rollte weiter, und der Mann folgte ihm. Endlich begegnete der Pfannkuchen einer Henne.

"Guten Morgen, Pfannkuchen," rief die Henne.

"Gott behüte Sie!" antwortete der Pfannkuchen.

"Ach, lieber Pfannkuchen!" rief die Henne. "Rollen Sie doch nicht so schnell. Warten Sie doch eine Minute, ich möchte Sie fressen."

"Ich kann nicht warten, ich muß weiter rollen," antwortete der Pfannkuchen, "denn die Frau mit den sieben hungrigen Kindern und der Mann wollen mich haben."

Und der Pfannkuchen rollte schnell weiter, und die Henne folgte ihm.

Dann begegnete der rollende Pfannkuchen einem Hahne.

"Guten Tag, lieber Pfannkuchen," rief der Hahn.

"Gott behüte Sie!" antwortete der Pfannkuchen und rollte weiter.

"Lieber Pfannkuchen," sagte der Hahn. "Warten Sie doch eine Minute. Ich möchte Sie fressen."

"Ich kann ja nicht warten," antwortete der Pfannkuchen, "ich muß weiter rollen, denn die Frau mit den sieben hungrigen Kindern, der Mann und die Henne folgen mir alle!"

Der Pfannkuchen rollte weiter, und der Hahn folgte ihm auch.

Dann begegnete der Pfannkuchen einer Ente.

"Guten Tag, Pfannkuchen," rief die Ente.

"Gott behüte Sie!" antwortete der Pfannkuchen.

"Aber, lieber Pfannkuchen, gehen Sie doch nicht so schnell!" rief die Ente. "Warten Sie. Ich möchte Sie fressen."

"Ich kann nicht warten!" antwortete der Pfannkuchen. "Da kommt die Frau mit den sieben hungrigen Kindern, der Mann, die Henne, der Hahn, und alle, alle wollen mich haben."

Der arme Pfannkuchen rollte weiter, und die Ente folgte ihm auch.

Endlich begegnete er einer Gans.

"Guten Tag, Pfannkuchen," rief die Gans.

"Gott behüte Sie!" antwortete der Pfannkuchen.

"Aber, lieber Pfannkuchen, rollen Sie doch nicht so schnell!" rief die Gans. "Warten Sie doch. Ich möchte Sie fressen!"

"Warten, ich kann nicht warten," antwortete der Pfannkuchen. "Da kommt die Frau mit den sieben hungrigen Kindern, der Mann, die Henne, der Hahn und die Ente, und alle wollen mich haben. Hier kann ich nicht bleiben. Ich muß weiter rollen!"

Der Pfannkuchen rollte weiter und die Gans lief ihm nach (folgte ihm).

Dann begegnete er einem Gänserich.

"Guten Tag, lieber Pfannkuchen!" rief der Gänserich.

"Gott behüte Sie!" antwortete der Pfannkuchen.

"Lieber Pfannkuchen, rollen Sie doch nicht so schnell!" rief der Gänserich. "Warten Sie eine Minute. Ich möchte Sie fressen!"

"Ach, ich kann ja nicht!" antwortete der Pfannkuchen. "Da kommt die Frau mit den sieben hungrigen Kindern, der Mann, die Henne, der Hahn, die Ente und die Gans, und alle, alle wollen mich haben. Darum kann ich nicht warten! Darum muß ich schnell weiter rollen!"

Und der Pfannkuchen rollte schnell weiter, und der Gänserich lief ihm nach.

Endlich begegnete der Pfannkuchen einem Schweine.

"Guten Tag, Pfannkuchen," sagte das Schwein.

"Gott behüte Sie!" antwortete der rollende Pfannkuchen.

"Warten Sie doch eine Minute, lieber Pfannkuchen!" rief das Schwein. "Ich möchte Sie fressen, und Sie gehen zu schnell."

"Ach, liebes Schwein, ich kann ja nicht warten. Die Frau mit den sieben hungrigen Kindern, der Mann, die Henne, der Hahn, die Ente, die Gans und der Gänserich kommen alle, um mich zu nehmen. Ich kann nicht warten." Und der Pfannkuchen rollte weiter und das Schwein lief ihm nach.

"Halt!" rief das Schwein. "Hier ist ein Wald, lieber Pfannkuchen. Im Walde sind nichts als Bäume. Da werden Sie sich fürchten!"

"Ja, das ist wahr (so)," antwortete der Pfannkuchen. "Im Walde, wo nichts als Bäume sind, werde ich mich fürchten."

"Gehen wir zusammen (beide) durch den Wald!" sagte das Schwein.

"Ach, ja, das ist ein guter Einfall!" rief der Pfannkuchen, und sie gingen zusammen.

Endlich kamen sie an einen Bach (ein sehr kleiner Strom). Das Schwein war so fett, daß es sehr gut schwimmen konnte. Aber der arme Pfannkuchen konnte nicht schwimmen. Dann sagte er zu dem Schweine: "Ach, mein lieber Freund, ich kann nicht schwimmen. Ich kann nicht über den Bach kommen!"

"Ach!" sagte das Schwein. "Es ist schade, daß Sie nicht schwimmen können. Aber springen Sie doch auf meinen Kopf, so werden Sie gut hinüber kommen."

"Das ist eine gute Idee!" sagte der Pfannkuchen, und er sprang auf den Kopf des Schweines.

Als das Schwein im Bach war, öffnete es den Mund und fraß den armen Pfannkuchen. Und, da der arme Pfannkuchen nicht weiter gehen konnte, so kann diese Geschichte auch nicht weiter gehen und muß hier enden.

English text:

Once upon a time, there was a woman who had seven hungry children. She made a pancake for the hungry kids. It was a big pancake, made of sweet milk, and she laid it in the pan on the fire.

The children who were so hungry were all standing there and the first child said: "Oh, mother, I'm so hungry, give me a piece of that pancake."

"Oh, good mother!" said the second child. "I'm also hungry, give me a piece of the pancake, too."

"Oh, dear, good mother!" said the third child. "I'm hungry, too. Give me a piece of the pancake."

"Oh, sweet, good, dear mother," said the fourth child. "I'm hungry, too. I'll have a piece of the pancake as well."

"Lovely, good, sweet, little mother," shouted (said aloud) the fifth child. "I want a piece of the pancake, too."

And the sixth child shouted: "Skillful, good, sweet, dear, little mother, let me also have a piece of the pancake. I'm hungry, too."

And the seventh and last child shouted: "Skillful, good, sweet, dear, cute, little mother, let me also have a piece of the pancake. I'm hungry, too."

"Yes, yes, my children," the woman replied. "Wait till the pancake's baked on the other side. Look, he is so beautiful and will be so good to eat."

When the cake heard that, he was very afraid and turned around quickly. Now he could also bake on the other side. After a few minutes, the pancake was baked, but because he was so afraid, he leaped right out of the pan. He jumped to the floor and quickly rolled out of the house.

"Stop, pancake, stop!" called the mother.

"Stop, pancake, stop!" the seven children shouted.

But the cake kept rolling fast. The wife and all seven children ran after him, but he rolled so fast that soon they could no longer see him. The pancake rolled on and on, and finally he met an old man.

"Hello, pancake!" the man shouted.

"God bless you!" replied the pancake.

"Don't roll so fast, dear pancake. Hold on, hold on. I want to eat you!"

"Alas!" answered the pancake. "I must hurry, for the woman with the seven hungry children are coming to eat me!"

And the pancake kept rolling, and the man followed him. Finally, the pancake met a hen.

"Good morning, pancake," the hen shouted.

"God bless you!" replied the pancake.

"Oh, dear pancake!" the hen shouted. "Don't roll so fast. Wait a minute, I want to eat you."

"I can't wait, I have to keep rolling," the pancake replied, "because the woman with the seven hungry children and the man want me."

And the pancake rolled on quickly, and the hen followed him.

Then the rolling pancake met a cockerel.

"Good day, dear pancake," the rooster shouted.

"God bless you!" the pancake replied and rolled on.

"Dear pancake," said the rooster. "Just wait a minute. I want to eat you."

"I can't wait," the pancake replied, "I have to keep rolling, because the woman with the seven hungry children, the man, and the hen are all following me!"

The pancake kept rolling, and the rooster followed.

Then the pancake met a duck.

"Hello, pancake," the duck shouted.

"God bless you!" replied the pancake.

"But, dear pancake, don't go so fast!" the duck shouted. "Wait, wait. I want to eat you."

"I can't wait!" replied the pancake. "Here comes the woman with the seven hungry children, the man, the hen, the rooster, and everyone, they all want me."

The poor pancake rolled on, and the duck followed him, too.

He met a goose.

"Hello, pancake," the goose shouted.

"God bless you!" replied the pancake.

"But, dear pancake, don't roll so fast!" the goose shouted. "Wait, please. I want to eat you!"

"Wait, I can't wait," the pancake replied. "Here comes the woman with the seven hungry children, the man, the hen, the rooster, and the duck, and they all want me. I can't stay here. I have to keep rolling!"

The pancake rolled on and the goose followed him.

Then he met a gander.

"Good day, dear pancake!" the gander shouted.

"God bless you!" replied the pancake.

"Dear pancake, don't roll so fast!" shouted the gander. "Wait a minute. I want to eat you!"

"Oh, I can't!" replied the pancake. "Here comes the woman with the seven hungry children, the man, the hen, the rooster, the duck, and the goose, and all of them want me. That's why I can't wait! I have to keep rolling!"

And the pancake rolled on quickly, and the gander ran after him.

Finally, the pancake met a pig

"Hello, pancake," said the pig.

"God bless you!" replied the pancake on wheels.

"Wait a minute, dear pancake!" the pig shouted. "I want to eat you, and you walk too fast."

"Oh, dear pig, I can't wait. The woman with the seven hungry children, the man, the hen, the cock, the duck, the goose, and the gander all come to take me. I can't wait." And the pancake kept rolling and the pig ran after him.

"Stop!" the pig shouted. "Here's a forest, dear pancake. There's nothing but trees in the forest. You'll be scared!"

"Yes, that's true," the pancake replied. "In the forest, where there are only trees, I will be afraid."

"Let's go together (both of us) through the forest!" said the pig.

"Oh, yeah, that's a good idea!" the pancake shouted, and they left together.

Finally, they came to a stream (a very small river). The pig was so fat that it could swim very well. But the poor pancake couldn't swim. Then he said to the pig: "Oh, my dear friend, I can't swim. I can't get across the creek!"

"Ah!" said the pig. "It's a pity you can't swim. Why don't you jump on my head and get across it with me?"

"That's a good idea!" said the pancake, and he jumped on the pig's head.

When the pig was in the creek, it opened its mouth and ate the poor pancake. And, since the poor pancake couldn't go any further, this story can't go any further and must end here.

Notes:

To end the series of stories on a humorous note, I've included the short story entitled "Der Pfannkuchen," which you have just read. Not only is this story remarkable in its Germanic gallows humor, deadpanning its way through a pancake's quest to get away from a family that wants to eat it, but it's also remarkable in the multitude of messages that can be taken from it.

The idea of a pancake, doomed from the onset to a destiny of being eaten, and running away from all its predators is one that is very dynamic. It's something of a Peter Pan story that has been told and retold in many different times and places. But a central theme that stays intact throughout all the different transcriptions is that the problems one faces always have a way of multiplying and eventually swallowing the sufferer whole if he or she simply runs away from them time and time again. Additionally, a pig helping a pancake cross a creek just isn't a great strategy for growth, however hilarious it may be.

One aspect of the German language which hasn't been discussed in depthly yet is the pronunciation of characters and words. While German is a very similar language to English and most of what is written in German can be pronounced naturally by an English speaker, there still remains some variance in pronunciation. Some pronunciation issues and examples the native English speaker often comes across are listed below.

The R sound: The sound of the German "r" is one of the sounds that lead listeners to judge that the language is ugly. It is produced by the medulla oblongata vibrating in the back of one's throat.

German, English: (Rot, Red), (Rose, Rose)

The V and W sounds: The V in German can actually produce two different sounds. One is similar to the F in German (and also in English). In essence, they have two letters which can produce the same sound (F).

German V pronounced as English F: (Vogel, Bird), (Vorsicht, Care)

Then again, the V can also share the same sound as the V in English (or, in German, a W). So the W and F sounds in German have two possibilities for expression, with W=V and F=V.

V pronounced like the English V: (Vase, Vase), (Klavier, Piano)

V pronounced like the English F: (Vetter, Cousin), (Vollmond, Full Moon)

The Umlaute ä, ö, ü: To most of us around the world who cannot claim German as our mother language, these sounds might prove to be the most challenging to pronounce. How one can pronounce a character that is not even found on most keyboards is the question here.

The "ä" is not too much of a struggle. However, when hearing both ä and e sounds spoken, it is not easy to distinguish between them. The short ä sounds like the E letter in the English words gender, men, or let.

The ö sound is quite close to the O sound in English, but with the former, the lips should be kept a little bit closer together. In fact, it makes the same sound one would when pronouncing fur, burden, or murder.

The ü may be the most challenging one to pronounce among those listed here because it has no close equivalent in the English language. Imagine if the English U were to meet a long ee: your lips are positioned as if you were about to whistle, yet instead of whistling, you then started to speak.

Some examples containing these three sounds are listed below:

Ä, ä: (ähnlich, similar), (Ärger, trouble)
Ö, ö: (öffentlich, public), (Öl, oil)
Ü, ü: (über, over), (Lüge, lie)

The SCH sound: These three letters form one sound in German, comparable with the English sh.

(Schöne, Nice), (Schuh, Shoe)

The CH sound: These two letters actually form one compound sound in the form of two different sounds in German; one is more and the other is less guttural. Few English words have a more guttural sound, and one of them is the famous Loch Ness. Remember the sound of ch in Loch as that is exactly what we are looking for.

More guttural ch: (Kachel, Tile), (Bach, Stream)

And then there is the ch sound that is less guttural. The difficulty here lies in the fact that there is nothing in English that this can be compared to. Try this: take the sound sh (as in shiver) and move the corners of your mouth outwards. You should come across a hissing sound, which should be something similar to the sounds of the following examples:

Less guttural ch: (Ich, I), (Gicht, Gout)

The SS/ß sound: Here, we once again come across an example of two different means of writing out one sound. Luckily for us, it's nothing too advanced. It's simply your standard "s" sound, as in sauce or song. But as every language does, the German language has a history, so while this character may be redundant, it is kept for the sake of tradition.

ss/ß: (Er hieß, his name was), (weiß, white)

Follow this orthographic rule for when to use which one of these spellings: After long diphthongs and long vowels, use ß; after short vowels, use ss.

What is a vowel?

Vowels in the German language constitute all the sounds which are not consonants (an explanation that is only marginally helpful, I admit), and they are also the letters that sound in of themselves. There are eight vowels in German: a, e, i, o, u, ä, ö, ü.

As you know, the sounds in between the vowels are consonants. Consonants can only be put together because of vowels, to an extent. Otherwise we would only have words like in the first example listed below. The second example is easy to pronounce, especially when compared to the first. Note that both examples are invented. They don't mean a thing (at least not in German).

Impossible to pronounce: Brgm
Easy to pronounce: Barogem

Short and long vowels

In German, just like in English, there are short vowels and there are long vowels. Some examples are listed below.

Short vowels: (Offen, Open), (Ass, Ace), (Suppe, Soup), (Bett, Bed), (Widder, Aries)

Long vowels: (Ofen, Oven), (Aas, Carrion), (Super, Super), (Beet, Flower bed), (Wieder, Again)

Some differences can be distinguished between these types of vowels. Between the pairs Ofen/Ofenn, Aas/Ass, Beet/Bett, and Widder/Wieder, there is one distinct difference: either the vowel is long or it is short. Their meanings are completely different though, and it is of great importance to know these differences. Short and long vowels are marked in certain ways in written German.

Ie *for long i*: (Wiese, Meadow), (Liegen, To lie down), (Wiegen, To weigh)
Aa *for long a*: (Aal, Eal), (Saal, Hall)

A vowel that is followed by an H becomes a long vowel: (Die Ahnen, Ancestors), (Etwas Ahnen, To suspect)
O: (Ohne, Without), (Ohr, Ear)
E: (Ehrliche, Honesty), (Ehre, Honor)

These examples do not contain any indication of whether the vowel is short or long: (Schaf, Sheep), (Laden, Shop), (Frage, Question)

If the vowel has a ß after it, then it will be long: (Straße, Street), (Stoß, Hit/Push), (Muße, Leisure)

A short vowel may be indicated by two consonants following it: (Immer, Always), (Essen, Eat), (Pass, Passport), (Müssen, To must)

Diphthongs (ei, ai, au): (Elmer, Bucket), (Seife, Soap), (Mai, May), (Sauer, Sour), (Bauer, Farmer), (Maus, Mouse)

The Z sound: Z in German makes the same sound as "ts" in English

(Zug, Train), (Ziehen, To pull), (Zeige, Goat)

The TZ sound: This sound is similar to the sound that Z makes. The main variance is a slight pronunciation of T.

Tz, Z: (Sitzen, To sit), (Siezen, To address someone formally), (Sitz, Seat), (Plütze, Puddle), (Platz, Place)

Note, however, that **ZT** is to be pronounced slightly differently: (Arzt, Doctor), (Er sitzt, He is sitting), (Er siezt uns, he formally addresses us)

Conclusion

Thank you for making it through to the end of *German Short Stories and Their English Translations*. I hope you enjoyed it and learned something along the way. Learning the German language (or any language, for that matter) is an endeavor that requires many hours of committed work if you are to reap any great rewards. The subject of German is one with a surface that cannot even be scratched within the narrow confines of these few pages. To properly learn German, the reader would need to continue to study, potentially for years. This book was meant to be a helpful guide for the beginner stages of the journey.

The reader's next step in his or her education would be to search for other resources to become more educated on the subject. The resources to be found are innumerable and are easily accessible. There are also some websites which provide side-by-side translations of texts in nearly all languages the world has to offer, all of which would be valuable assets to the reader moving forward.

Some tips to keep in mind when learning a new language would be to know what your goal is, as it is much easier to stay motivated when you have a clear purpose for what you are doing. You must also be clear on what the topic has to offer to you as the student. Speak with a partner or just with yourself for practice. Doing this can help you discover, refresh, and retain words and phrases in your mind, as well as build confidence in your abilities to reach your goal. Listen to the language as spoken by a native; make certain words and phrases concrete in your mind using repetition and familiarity.

Most importantly of all, have fun! You won't want language-learning to become just another chore.

Finally, if you found this book useful in any way, a review on Amazon would be greatly appreciated!

www.ingramcontent.com/pod-product-compliance
Lightning Source LLC
Chambersburg PA
CBHW052206110526
44591CB00012B/2105